STEP-UP Books

are written especially for children who have outgrown beginning readers. In this exciting series:

- the words are harder (but not too hard)
- there's more text (but it's still in big print)
- there are plenty of illustrations (but the books aren't picture books)
- the subject matter has been carefully chosen to appeal to young readers who want to find out about the world around them. They'll love these informative and lively books.

DAREDEVILS DO AMAZING THINGS

Here is a fascinating collection of five true hold-your-breath stories about American daredevils and their death-defying feats. There's Blondin, who walked on a tightrope across Niagara Falls—carrying a man on his back; Annie Oakley, who shot a cigarette from the mouth of Crown Prince Wilhelm of Germany; and Evel Knievel, who tried to jump across the mile-wide Snake River Canyon in his Sky-Cycle. Other stories include a fight with a giant octopus and one of Harry Houdini's famous escapes.

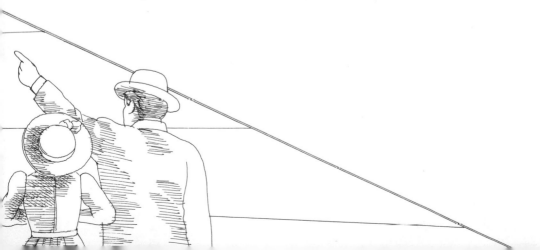

DAREDEVILS Do

by Robert Kraske
illustrated by Ivan Powell

Step-Up Books ⎍ Random House
New York

Library of Congress Cataloging in Publication Data
Kraske, Robert. Daredevils do amazing things. (Step-up books; 26) SUMMARY: Describes the five daring feats of adventurers Blondin, Harry Houdini, Annie Oakley, Harry Rieseberg and Evel Knievel. 1. Entertainers—United States—Biography—Juvenile literature. 2. Houdini, Harry, 1874–1926—Juvenile literature. 3. Oakley, Annie, 1860–1926—Juvenile literature. 4. Rieseberg, Harry Earl—Juvenile literature. 5. Knievel, Evel, 1938–   —Juvenile literature. 6. Blondin, Jean François Gravelet, known as, 1824–1897—Juvenile literature. [1. Adventure and adventurers] I. Powell, Ivan. II. Title. GV1811.A1K7   791'.092'2   [B]   [920] 77-90194   ISBN 0-394-83623-5   ISBN 0-394-93623-X lib. bdg.

Manufactured in the United States of America   1 2 3 4 5 6 7 8 9 0

Contents

The Greatest Tightrope Walker in the World

Blondin was the greatest tightrope walker
in the world. In June 1859, he came to
Niagara Falls. Below the falls, water churned
between cliffs 240 feet high.

"Here is the place," he said. "This is where I shall walk over the river on my tightrope!"

No one believed he could do it.

"Walk over the river on a rope? Don't be foolish!"

"You will fall!"

"You will kill yourself!"

But Blondin did not listen. Calmly he went ahead with his plans. First, he tied the tightrope to strong oak trees. The trees stood on the cliffs high above the river. Then he tied thin guy ropes every 20 feet along the tightrope.

"I don't want the wind to blow the tightrope and make me slip," he told people watching him. "These guy ropes will hold the tightrope steady."

On June 30, Blondin was ready.

Thousands of people came to watch him. They brought picnic baskets. Some sat in trees. They all wanted to see Blondin. Was he a brave man—or a very foolish man? Everyone looked over the rock cliffs at the white water boiling far below. And everyone asked the same question: "Do you think he will fall?"

Suddenly a boy in a tree yelled, "There
he is!"

Everyone looked. Sure enough, Blondin was
stepping out from the cliff onto the tightrope.
He was carrying a 38-foot pole to help him
balance.

People could hardly believe what they saw.
Blondin began RUNNING along the rope. In
the center, he stopped and waved. People
laughed and cheered.

Then Blondin began to do tricks.
First, he did a back flip.
Next he hung by one leg.
Then he walked backwards
and balanced on one foot.
Finally he stood on his head
and kicked his legs.

When he finished his tricks,
he walked back to the cliff.
People sighed. "Ahh!
He made it!"

Each day more people came to Niagara Falls to see Blondin perform, and each day his tricks became more daring. He walked on stilts. He walked with baskets tied to his feet. He rode a bicycle. He even pushed a wheelbarrow along the thin rope.

One day he took a table, chair, and basket out on the tightrope. He balanced the table. Then he took a cake and a bottle of wine from the basket and set them on the table. But as he was about to sit on the chair, it slipped!

People jumped to their feet and cried out! They watched the chair tumble through the sunshine-filled air. Down—down it went—until it became a dot and splashed—a tiny splash—into the roaring river below.

And Blondin? He laughed and waved. Then he sat on the tightrope and ate the cake and drank the wine!

"How do you do it?" people asked. "How can you walk along a thin rope? Why don't you ever fall?"

"I shall tell you my secret," Blondin said. "I keep looking at the rope 20 feet ahead. Sometimes I whistle or hum a song. And if a person has perfect balance as I do, what is there to be scared about?"

All summer Blondin walked the tightrope. Trains brought people from miles around to watch. "Someday," everyone said, "he will surely lose his balance."

And on August 19 that's exactly what happened. Blondin did lose his balance—high above the Niagara River—but in a way he never expected.

On that afternoon he was trying a new trick. For this trick, Blondin had big signs painted:

> ON THIS DAY, I, BLONDIN,
> THE GREATEST
> TIGHTROPE WALKER IN THE
> WORLD,
> WILL CARRY A BRAVE MAN
> ON MY BACK
> ACROSS THE NIAGARA RIVER!

Crowds came early that day to see the new trick. But Blondin had one problem. No one wanted to cross the tightrope with him. Everyone said, "Oh, no! Not me, thank you! Please find someone else."

By late afternoon, people waiting on the cliffs were growing restless. And still Blondin had not found anyone to cross the tightrope with him.

At last he turned to his friend Harry Colcord. "Harry, you will have to come with me."

"Me!" Harry's face turned white.

"I promised the people," Blondin said.

"Maybe YOU did, but I didn't!" Harry said.

Blondin looked long and hard at him. "Are you my friend?"

"Yes."

"Do you trust me?"

"Yes."

"Did I ever fall off the tightrope?"

"N-no."

"Harry, I need you."

Colcord took a deep breath. He looked at the tightrope—it stretched like a thin pencil line between the cliffs. Then he looked at the waiting people. He tried to keep his voice steady.

"All right. I'll go with you."

Harry Colcord was a very brave man.

Blondin placed a rope loop over each of his shoulders. Harry climbed on Blondin's back, put a leg through each loop, and wrapped his arms around Blondin's neck.

"Don't hold on so tight!" Blondin gasped. "You are choking me! I can't breathe!"

"Oh," Harry said, looking at the river far below. "Sorry." He loosened his hold.

"That's better," Blondin said, rubbing his neck. "Now listen to me. Sit very still—don't move. And whatever you do, don't look down."

Harry tried to swallow, but his mouth felt sticky and dry. "All—all right," he said.

Blondin picked up his balancing pole and stepped out on the rope. Harry closed his eyes. Quickly Blondin ran to the center. Then he stopped.

"You are too heavy!" he said. "I'm getting tired! You will have to get off my back!"

Harry's eyes popped open. "Get off your back?"

He looked at the faraway cliff. He looked down at the river far below. All around was empty air. A cool breeze blew against his cheek. Only the thin rope stretched ahead.

Harry felt dizzy. "Where should I go?" He could not think of anything else to say.

"Never mind!" Blondin gasped. "Just get off my back! I need to rest!"

Slowly—carefully—Harry lifted one leg out of the rope loop hanging from Blondin's shoulder. His foot felt for the tightrope. Then he lifted his other leg out of the loop. He stood on the rope, one foot behind the other, one arm around Blondin's neck. His stomach turned. He felt sick.

"That's better!" Blondin said. He took deep
breaths. The ends of the long balancing pole
slowly dipped and rose as he rested. Then:
"Harry, don't hold so tight!"

"I can't help it! I'm scared!"

"Harry, if you don't let up, I shall walk
away and leave you!"

Harry's mouth opened. "Leave me? Up here in—in the sky? Oh, no!"

But he let up on his hold.

Finally, Blondin was rested. "All right. Climb back onto my shoulders."

On the cliffs, the people watched Harry carefully climb onto Blondin's back. Except for the faraway roar of the river, not a sound could be heard. A few people placed their hands over their eyes and turned away.

Then Blondin started walking again. He was puffing hard. Colcord was too heavy.

Slowly they came to one of the thin guy ropes holding the tightrope. Blondin stopped. "I'm going to rest. Stay where you are."

He placed one foot on the guy rope to steady himself.

SNAP! The rope broke!

Blondin and Harry teetered. They tipped one way and then the other. Blondin tried to balance himself with the pole. Harry clung to his back.

On the cliffs, women screamed. Men jumped to their feet.

"They are going to fall!" someone yelled.

For a long moment, Blondin swayed. The cliffs and sky dipped and rose before Harry's frightened eyes. He clung to Blondin's twisting shoulders. The long pole swung up and down.

Then—slowly—Blondin found his balance. Carefully he stood straight. Harry could feel Blondin's heart thumping hard.

Blondin started walking again. Carefully he placed one foot in front of the other. Slowly . . . slowly . . . he made his way to the far cliff. At last! He stepped off the rope and onto solid ground.

They were safe!

People cheered. "Hurrah! Hurrah for Blondin!"

Harry sat on the cool grass. His knees felt weak.

Blondin patted his friend's shoulder. "You are a very brave man, Harry."

Harry Colcord never went out on the tightrope again. But Blondin went right on doing his tricks for the people at Niagara Falls.

For many years—until he was 72 years old—Blondin walked the tightrope in circuses all over the world.

Never once did he slip.

Never once did he fall, because . . .

He was Blondin, the greatest tightrope walker in the world!

Escape from a Box—Underwater!

July 7, 1912. A tugboat chugged into New York harbor. On deck, Harry Houdini stood next to a wooden box. The box was made of boards. It was two feet wide, three feet high, and three feet long. The top was off.

"I'm ready!" Houdini said to newspaper reporters watching him. "Put the top on!" He was wearing a bathing suit. He stepped into the box and sat down.

Reporters placed the top on the box. "Give me a hammer," said one. Carefully, he pounded nails around the top. "There!" he said. "The top is on tight! Houdini will never get out!"

"Here is a rope," said another reporter. "Tie it around the box. Tight!"

"Is everyone ready?" said a third reporter. "O.K.! Into the water with it!"

The reporters pushed the box off the deck and into the water. SPLASH! "There goes Houdini!"

The box sank fast. Bubbles came to the top of the water.

"He will never get out of there," a reporter said.

"I wonder why he risks his life like this?" asked another reporter.

Houdini was a magician. He liked to do tricks. He liked to amaze people. For many years, he performed in theaters in America and Europe. On one stage, he made an elephant step into a huge box—and disappear! On another stage, workmen built a brick wall for Houdini. He walked right through the wall! At least, that's what people said. But he didn't really walk through the wall. He just made people THINK he did. It was all a trick.

Houdini also did escape tricks. He walked into a jail cell. The door was closed and locked. Eight minutes later he walked out. Another time he sat down in a steel safe. The door was closed and locked. Fourteen minutes later he stepped out. He escaped from coffins, an iron tank, and a milk can filled with water. He also let people lock him in chains and handcuffs. He always got out.

"How does he do it?" people asked.

"Easy!" said some know-it-alls. "Houdini is magic! He can change himself into smoke! Then he passes through tiny holes and cracks. That's how he escapes!"

Houdini did not like to hear this. "I'm not magic!" he said. "No one is. I have ways to escape. But magic is not one of them!"

On July 7, he told people that he would escape from a box. Where would the box be? At the bottom of New York harbor. There, in the cold, dark water, he would make his escape.

"What if you can't get out?" a reporter asked Houdini. "There must be an easier way to die!"

Hundreds of people came to the harbor that day. "Houdini is foolish!" many said. "He will surely drown!"

But Houdini did not plan to drown. For one thing, he had practiced holding his breath under water. In his bathtub at home, he could hold his breath for four minutes and 16 seconds! That's a long time! Most people have a hard time holding their breath even ONE minute!

Exactly 57 seconds after the box splashed into the water, Houdini came to the surface. He waved an arm. Reporters on the tugboat saw him.

"There he is!"
"He's O.K.!"

They pulled Houdini out of the water. Then they lifted the box back on deck.

"Look!" everyone said. "The top is still on the box! The nails have not been pulled out! The rope is still tied around it! How did he escape?"

What people didn't know was that Houdini
had planned his escape well. He always made
sure he could escape BEFORE he stepped into a
safe, a jail cell, or a coffin. This time he had
used a box made of boards. One board was
not fixed firmly in place. The nails pounded
into it were short—only half an inch long.
They didn't go all the way through the board.
Two secret metal tabs held the board in place.

As the box sank, Houdini used a thin strip
of steel to open the tabs. He pulled the board
in. Then he squeezed through the opening.
Outside the box, he pulled the board back in
place. Then he swam up. The box came up
behind him. The top was still in place. The
rope was still around it.

No one ever guessed how Houdini escaped. "He must be magic!" people said. "He can pass through the wall of a box!"

That was the only way they could explain it.

"The secret of my magic," Houdini said, "is not WHAT I do, but what people THINK I do. After all, everyone loves a good mystery!"

A good mystery, indeed—but still a very dangerous trick.

Inside the box, in the darkness and cold water, if the tabs had stuck . . . if the board had not opened . . .

Little Sure Shot

In 1875, Frank Butler came to Ohio. He was a sharpshooter. "I can shoot better than any man!" he told people who came to see his show. "Here is the prize!" He held up money. "Who can beat me? Who wants to try?"

"I do!" a small voice said. Annie Oakley stepped onto the stage. She was 15 years old.

"A girl!" Frank Butler said. "Why, you aren't big enough to hold a gun!"

Annie Oakley was just five feet tall. She weighed a hundred pounds. She had long brown hair, dark brown eyes and a warm smile. She held a rifle. "Let's shoot!"

A man threw small glass balls into the air, one at a time. Frank shot. Then Annie shot. When the contest was over, Frank had hit 24. Annie had hit 25!

Frank was surprised. "Little girl," he said, "you are a better shot than I am! You win the prize. Here is the money."

Annie needed that money. Her family was very poor. She lived in a log cabin with her mother and six brothers—her father was dead. To help put food on the table, Annie began to hunt. She hunted rabbits and squirrels. With so much practice, she became the best rifle shot around her home. Farmers came to watch her shoot. She could hit pennies and stones tossed in the air. The farmers called her "Little Sure Shot."

The shooting contest with Frank Butler had another ending. Years later, Annie and Frank were married. They joined Buffalo Bill's Wild West Show. Annie rode a horse and shot flying glass balls. Frank held up a penny. Annie shot it away. Frank dropped a playing card. Annie shot five holes in it before it hit the ground. He held up the ace of clubs. She shot a hole right through the center. Did she ever miss? Yes, but not very often.

There was one shot that people always enjoyed. They smiled as she called, "Come here, Dave." Dave was her pet dog. She set an apple on his head. "Now sit still."

Annie walked back 30 steps. She aimed very carefully. She pulled the trigger. BANG! The apple flew off Dave's head. His tail wagged. People said, "If I ever saw a dog smile, it was surely Dave!"

Annie wanted to become the best sharpshooter in the world. In 1885, she broke 4,772 out of 5,000 glass balls to beat the record of Frank Carver. He called himself the "Champion Shot of the World." Annie was now the best sharpshooter. No one could beat her.

Buffalo Bill's Wild West Show went to England. The year was 1887. Queen Victoria came to see Annie shoot. After the show, the Queen spoke to Annie. "You are a very clever little girl." She gave Annie a medal. English newspapers called her "Annie Oakley of the Magic Gun!"

Later that year, Crown Prince Wilhelm of Germany invited Annie to his country. The show took place at the Charlottenburg Race Course, near Berlin. Princes and generals came to watch. Prince Wilhelm wore a beautiful white uniform. Many medals hung on his chest. "Begin the show!" he said.

Annie shot clay birds and flying glass balls. She threw six balls into the air. She picked up six rifles—one at a time—and hit every ball before it hit the ground.

Then something happened that Annie
didn't expect. Prince Wilhelm walked up to
her. He lighted a cigarette and put it between
his lips. He pointed to the glowing tip. "Shoot
it out!"

Annie bit her lip. She really did not want to
try this shot. There might be an accident. She
could hurt—even kill—the next ruler of
Germany. Yet she could not say no. If
she did, she would no longer be Little Sure
Shot, the best sharpshooter in the world.

The day was gray and cloudy, the wind
cold. The princes and generals watched. Their
eyes were as hard as stone. Their eyes said,
"Annie, you had better not miss!"

Slowly Annie walked 30 steps from the
prince. She looked down the rifle. She saw the
side of Wilhelm's head. She saw the red tip of
the cigarette. Should she press the trigger?
Not many shooters would dare such a shot. If
she missed . . .

BANG! Wilhelm's head jerked back. Only a
short stub of cigarette stayed between his lips.

The princes and generals clapped. They
were smiling. Wilhelm shook Annie's hand.
"Wunderbar!" he said. "Wonderful!"

Annie had dared to make the hardest shot
of her life. She was still Little Sure Shot, the
finest sharpshooter in the world.

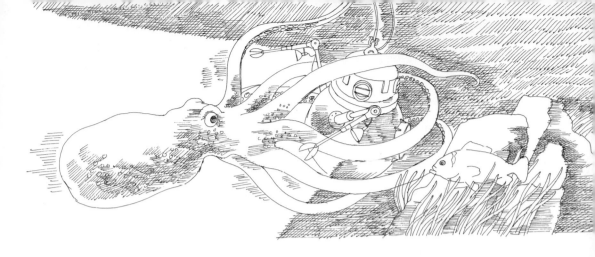

The Man Who Fought a Sea Monster—
and Won!

Harry Rieseberg was a treasure hunter. He went down to the bottom of the sea. He looked for gold and silver in sunken ships. These ships once carried treasure from South America to Spain. On the ocean, storms sank the ships. With them went the treasure.

Diving for treasure is exciting. It is also very dangerous. Divers cannot breathe in water. They must carry tanks of air. If something goes wrong with the tank and a diver cannot breathe, he dies.

Divers also face other dangers when they look for treasure. Harry Rieseberg met sharks. Sometimes he had to fight them. Sharks have very sharp teeth. A shark could have bitten off Harry's leg. It could have killed him, too.

Harry once met another kind of underwater animal- a monster octopus. It had eight long arms. It was big enough and strong enough to hold Harry underwater until his air ran out. Here is what happened.

The year was 1935. Harry was in Peru, in South America. He was looking for a sunken ship called the *Santa Cruz*. The *Santa Cruz* had sunk 250 years before. It carried 30 million pieces of gold!

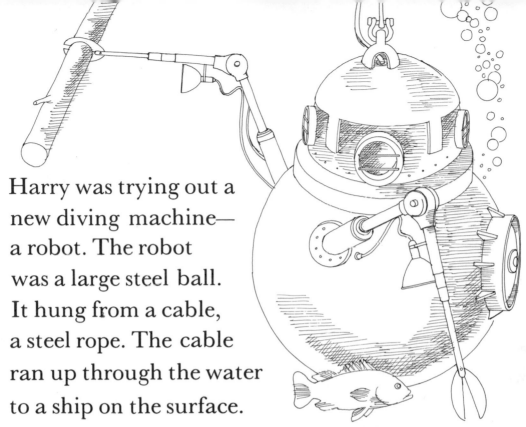

Harry was trying out a new diving machine— a robot. The robot was a large steel ball. It hung from a cable, a steel rope. The cable ran up through the water to a ship on the surface.

The robot had long arms with steel claws. The claws could pick up a gold piece on the ocean floor. They were also strong and sharp enough to cut a log in two.

Inside the robot, Harry could look through windows and move the arms. He could also talk on a telephone to helpers on the ship above.

On the sea floor, Harry saw an old ship. "We have found the treasure ship!" he called on the telephone.

Twenty feet from Harry was his friend Gomez. Gomez was in a diving bell. It looked like a hot-water tank with windows. Gomez had a movie camera. His job was to take pictures of Harry in the robot moving around the old ship.

"Gomez!" Harry called into his phone. "Can you see me? I'm ready to move into the old ship. I hope a money chest is inside!"

"Good luck, Harry!" Gomez called back. "I have you on camera!"

Suddenly, Harry saw something move in the water. It was behind Gomez's diving bell. Then he saw what it was—a giant octopus creeping out of a dark cave.

Harry had never seen a monster octopus like this one. Its arms were as thick as telephone poles. Its eyes were as large as grapefruits. Gomez didn't see it. It moved toward the diving bell. One of its long arms reached out. It felt the bell, then pulled back. It reached out again.

Harry felt cold drops of sweat run down his sides. "Gomez!" he called into the phone. "Watch out! Octopus!"

But it was too late. Three of the monster's arms were wrapped around the diving bell. Harry knew the monster would never let go. Gomez would run out of air. He would die.

"What can I do?" Harry thought. The monster seemed angry. It pulled the bell close and shook it. Then it lifted the bell and smashed it down. Harry could hear the metal bell bang on the rocks. The sound came right through the water. BANG! BANG! BANG!

"Gomez!" he called. "Are you all right? Can you hear me!"

There was no answer.

Harry knew he had to do something. The monster was now swinging the bell against the rocks. Harry called to the ship above. "Move me closer to the diving bell!"

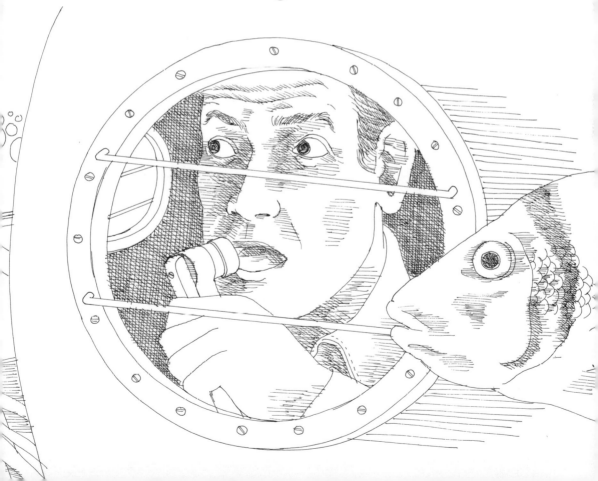

Harry opened one of the robot's steel claws. With it he grabbed one of the octopus's arms. The sharp claw cut into the arm. It cut through the flesh like a knife cutting through a watermelon. The monster octopus twisted and turned.

Harry cut through a second arm—then a third. The octopus tried to wrap an arm around the robot. If the octopus held the robot's arms, then Harry could not use them. One of the monster's eyes blinked and looked at Harry. Harry felt like screaming. The eye looked as large as a dinner plate.

Then—slowly—the eye closed. Harry
watched amazed as the monster sank to the
bottom.

Harry called on the phone. "Pull us up!"

On the ship, in the warm sun, men pulled
Gomez from the bell. He had cuts on his arms
and bumps on his head. "Oooooh . . ." he
groaned and rubbed his head. Gomez was
alive!

That afternoon, Harry and Gomez went down to the sea bottom again. Harry left the robot on the ship. He wanted to see the monster octopus close up. He was in a diving suit. Gomez was in the bell.

They found the dead monster. Gomez took pictures of Harry standing next to it. From arm tip to arm tip, it was 24 feet across! A VERY big octopus!

In the old ship, Harry found a chest. He tied a rope around it. Helpers pulled it up. In the sun again, Harry opened the chest. Inside was $40,000 in gold bars and coins.

No, the ship was not the *Santa Cruz*. It was another treasure ship. Harry never learned its name. But he had its gold. And to get it, he had fought a sea monster— and won!

The Greatest Daredevil?

Who is the greatest daredevil of all? Who has done the largest number of brave and reckless things? Many people would name Evel Knievel. Evel does dangerous stunts with a motorcycle. People all over the world watch him on TV.

Evel starts at the top of a high runway. He speeds down. Then he "flies" his motorcycle over something. He has jumped over a pile of 51 cars. He has jumped over 13 big trucks parked side by side. He has jumped over 21 cars parked side by side. He has jumped over a pool of man-eating sharks.

Once he jumped over a line of boxes. The boxes held poisonous rattlesnakes. His motorcycle hit the last box. It broke open, and 50 rattlesnakes crawled out. People ran! They didn't want to share their seats with rattlesnakes!

Evel has made more than 300 jumps on a motorcycle. But he has not always landed safely. He has crashed at least 12 times. He has broken about 50 bones. In his right hip he has a steel plate in place of bone. He walks with a kind of stiff limp.

People often ask Evel why he risks his life. This is what he once said:

"I like to live with a lump in my throat and a knot in my stomach."

The jump Evel is best known for took place in 1974. He told people he would jump a motorcycle over a canyon. A canyon is a deep and wide opening in the earth—such as the Grand Canyon. The sides are high rock walls.

The canyon Evel wanted to jump was the Snake River Canyon, in Idaho. It is almost a mile wide. The rock walls are 600 feet high. Far, far down at the bottom flows the Snake River.

On Sunday, September 8, twenty thousand people came to the canyon. They came to see Evel "fly" across it. In theaters in the United States, and in Europe and Asia, thousands more watched huge TV screens. People saw Evel in a red, white, and blue jumpsuit. They watched him walk to the Sky-Cycle X–2. It sat on a ramp 108 feet long. The ramp was pointed at the sky over the canyon.

For this jump across the canyon, Evel decided not to use a motorcycle. Instead, he built the Sky-Cycle, a special airplane. Inside the Sky-Cycle was a tank holding 500 pounds of water. The water was heated to 700 degrees Fahrenheit. It became super-hot steam trying to get out of the tank. When Evel pushed a red button, the steam would rush out the back of the tank. This rush of steam would push the Sky-Cycle up the ramp and into the sky at 400 miles per hour. The Sky-Cycle would zoom to 3,000 feet over the canyon.

At the back end of the Sky-Cycle X–2 were two cans. One can held a small parachute. The second can held a large parachute. High over the canyon, Evel planned to pull a handle. The small parachute would come out of its can. It would pull the large parachute out of its can.

The large parachute would cause the
X–2 to float down. It would land on the cliff
at the opposite side of the canyon. At least,
that is what Evel HOPED would happen.

But no one really knew if the Sky-Cycle
would take Evel across the canyon. Two other
Sky-Cycles—not carrying anyone—had
crashed. Evel had watched them being tested.
One flew off the ramp and fell into the
canyon. It smashed on rocks beside the river.
The second one had dropped into the river.

Would the Sky-Cycle with Evel inside make
it? Would it fly all the way across the canyon?
Everyone was waiting to see what would
happen.

Evel sat down in the Sky-Cycle. He put on
his crash helmet. He strapped on his seat belt.

A wind blew fine dust. The people became
quiet.

Evel's left hand held the parachute handle. His right hand rested on the red button. The countdown began . . .

. . . 6 . . . 5 . . . 4 . . . 3 . . . 2 . . . 1 . . .

Blast-off!

A white burst of steam shot from the Sky-Cycle. "It was as loud as a dragon's roar!" said one reporter. Dust and rocks blew away behind it.

The Sky-Cycle X–2
zoomed up the ramp.
Evel's head pushed
back into the seat. But even
before the X–2 came off the
ramp, something went wrong.
The small parachute popped
out of its can. It made the Sky-Cycle
lose speed. Did that mean the X–2 could not
carry Evel all the way across the canyon?

The Sky-Cycle went
1,400 feet into the sky.
It kept spinning and
rolling all the way.
Then it stopped going up.
It began to fall. Down,
down, down.

"He's going to crash into
the river!" people called.

Then they yelled again.
"Look! Look!" The small
parachute had pulled the
large parachute out of its can.
The large 'chute slowed the
Sky-Cycle's fall.
Now it was falling between
the rock walls—right for the river!
If it landed in deep water,
Evel would surely drown!

The Sky-Cycle fell nose down. It fell as slowly as a leaf falling from a tree. A wind pushed it, pushed it again. It bumped against the rock wall of the canyon. Down, down . . .

The Sky-Cycle splashed into one foot of water near the shore of the Snake River. It missed deep water by only a few feet. Two men in a boat came quickly to the Sky-Cycle. They cut Evel's seat belt and pulled him out.

A helicopter flew Evel back to the top of the cliff. Newspaper reporters crowded around. "What went wrong, Evel? What happened?"

Evel shook his head. "I don't know." His face and nose were scratched. But he was not hurt. "The cycle went sideways. I could see the canyon wall coming at me." He was very pale. "I am the luckiest man in the world!"

Evel had come close to being killed. But he was used to that. Risking his life was his work.

More people have watched Evel Knievel than any other daredevil. Does this make him the greatest daredevil of all? What do YOU think?

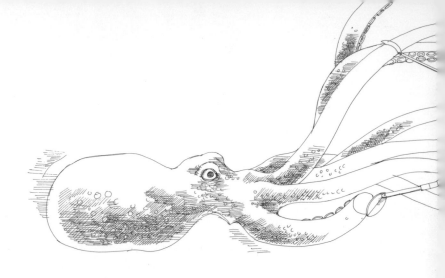

ABOUT THE AUTHOR

Robert Kraske has spent many years writing and editing magazine articles and books for children. Among other subjects, he has written about pirates, Harry Houdini (a famous magician), Benedict Arnold (an infamous Revolutionary War general), the patriotic songs we sing, the Statue of Liberty, burglar alarms, messages in seagoing bottles, and life in outer space. Mr. Kraske lives in Stillwater, Minnesota, with his wife and three children.

ABOUT THE ILLUSTRATOR

Ivan Powell, a former advertising art director, is presently a teacher of illustration and editorial design at Syracuse University as well as a free-lance illustrator for magazine and book publishers. As if that weren't enough, he is also the designer and builder of a unique 20-foot Elephant Slide for children.

Mr. Powell, who grew up in New York City, now lives in Syracuse, New York. *Daredevils Do Amazing Things* is the first full-length children's book he has illustrated.